PRESENTATIONS

PRESENTATIONS

A Passion for Gift Wrapping

Carolyne Roehm

Photographed by Sylvie Becquet

and Antonis Achilleos

Also by Carolyne Roehm
At Home with Carolyne Roehm
Carolyne Roehm Spring Notebook
Carolyne Roehm Winter Notebook
Carolyne Roehm Fall Notebook
Carolyne Roehm Summer Notebook
A Passion for Flowers

Broadway Books, New York

Book design by
Doug Turshen & David Huang

Printed in China

BROADWAY BOOKS and its logo, a letter B bisected on the diagonal, are trademarks of Random House, Inc. Visit our website at **www.broadwaybooks.com.** First edition published 2005.

Cataloging-in-Publication Data is on file with the Library of Congress

ISBN 0-7679-2112-7
10 9 8 7 6 5 4 3 2 1

Thank You!

As with all of my projects, I wish to acknowledge the help of my staff. Thank you to Rosa Costa, who organizes my life and helps me with a million details. To Placido and Margarida de Carvalho for their tireless efforts and help with everything I do. To Leila Aquino, who spent hours helping me muddle through the computer labyrinth as we worked on our wrapping paper designs.

A thank you to Doug Turshen for his support, belief in my projects, and design talent in laying out my books. His graphic designer, David Huang, gets my thanks, too.

As always, a big thank you to my friend Sylvie Becquet: You are my alter ego and capture all that I do in your beautiful photographs.

A thank you to my editors Jennifer Josephy and Donna Bulseco, who make my run-on sentences into intelligible text. Thank you to my witty friend Sharon King Hoge for coming up with the title of this book.

Thank you to my agent Cullen Stanley for presenting my work to publishers and helping me make sound decisions.

Thank you to Mom, Mittie Ann, and Simon for their loving support.

Finally, thank you, Grandma Beaty, for instilling your love of a prettily wrapped package in me.

Carolyne Roehm

MILLENNIUM

MST

Ms. Carolyne Roehm

NAME
DESTINATION

CONTA

PIECES O

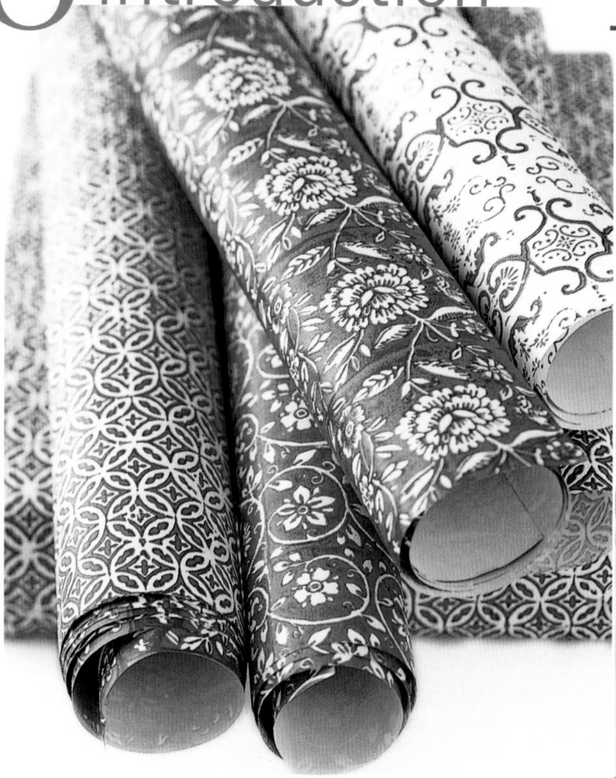

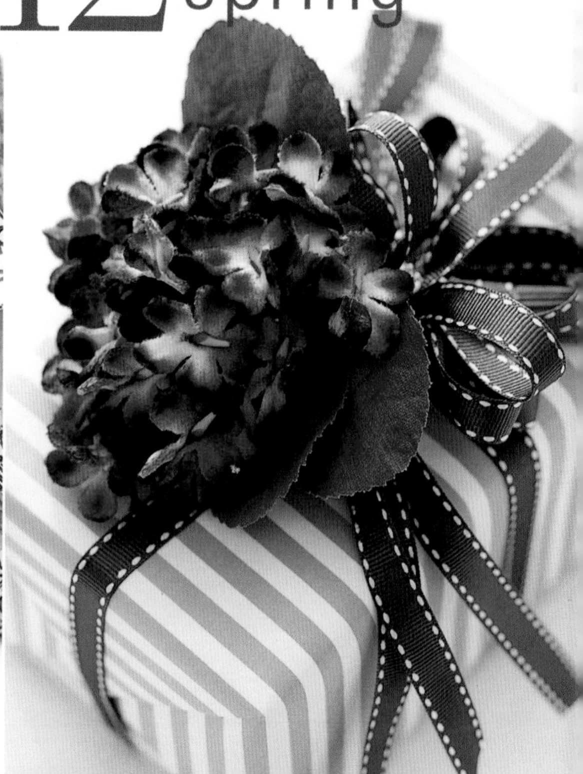

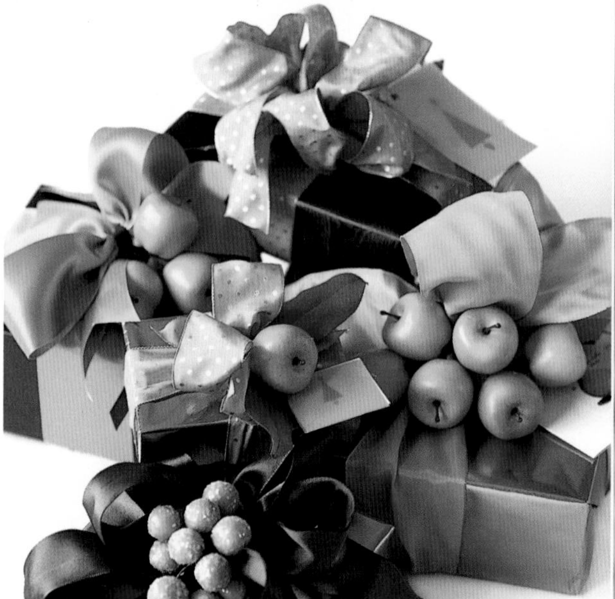

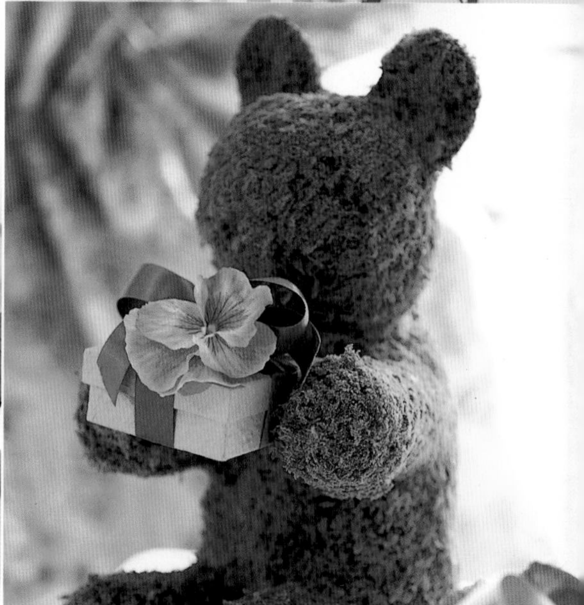

I have always loved wrapping pretty packages. Like so many of my other passions—flowers, gardening, decorating, and entertaining—it is a form of self-expression that was cultivated in me at a very young age by my grandmother. Her collection of antique ribbons, her ideas, and scrupulous attention to details were a source of inspiration and education. For me, creating a beautifully wrapped package is fun and pleasurable, and always adds to the enjoyment of a festive occasion. What follows is designed to inspire and delight you to try your hand at what can be a satisfying pursuit.

Take a moment to look through these pages before you wrap your next gift. I hope the ideas presented here will be a springboard for your creativity. I often speak about inspiration; this is not merely a reference to one's creative powers (which is a complex subject), but instead something much simpler and more direct. Inspiration often comes from observing; we must remember to keep our eyes open and pay attention to details. Honing those skills is important in learning how to design. I have noticed that while many of us say we "see" something, we in fact only glance at it. When I design a package, I start by studying a line, a motif, or a combination of colors in order to create something new.

You will notice that I may use a design or a motif or a color combination over and over. I do this not because I do not have another idea but because these are constants in my design vocabulary. You too will discover things that you love and use often. That is great! It means you are in the process of creating your style. The trick to creativity is to take the constants in your design lexicon and reinvent them. Every designer does this; it is how she or he establishes a "look." In my gift wraps, I use things I make as well as ones I purchase. It is not always necessary to re-create the wheel when there are many lovely designs available. These can become your own through how you use them. Remember, a great editor is yet another kind of creator.

I have many sources of inspiration. Because I am a gardener, nature has always been an influence with its seasonal colors and rich textures. As John Ruskin eloquently said, "There is material enough in a single flower for the ornament of a score of cathedrals." Travel is another source. Visiting places and absorbing the artistic detail in other cultures enables us to broaden our aesthetic scope. We learn by observing how others live, what they celebrate, eat, or wear, and by studying their art, architecture, textiles, and sense of color. Traveling is also an opportunity to collect. Scouring bazaars, flea markets, and shops has fueled my longtime hobby of collecting materials, from a roll of brocade ribbon from India or paper from Japan to straw ornaments from South America and velvet flowers from France. Some treasures I have saved for years, knowing the right time and occasion will come along to use them.

Great art is also a source of inspiration. From the Old Masters to today's modern masters, we have much to learn by studying their sense of color, line, light, texture, and composition. We can make use of facsimiles of their work found in museum shops when wrapping gifts.

I have shared with you the reasons I like wrapping presents, my personal sources for inspiration, and some favorite ideas. I hope this book gives you the ability to define those things for yourself, and in the process, to bring a small joy, a memory, or simply a moment of pleasure to you and to someone you love.

...for me, creating a pretty package

is a form of self-expression.

Spring is a gift to our spirit and creativity. The wealth of inspiration that comes from this wonderful time of year is unlimited. After the gray days of a long winter, we welcome the fresh air, the warm sun, and all of the beautiful flowers that unexpectedly bloom. What better incentive to create and decorate! After all, who wouldn't love a present that came with a nosegay of spring violets nestled in a sumptuous bow? No one I know!

Take in spring's shimmering greens, apple blossom pinks, and delicate lilacs, and refresh your imagination with a lifetime of ideas.

Spring colors are like
sorbets—cool, refresh-
ing, and irresistible.
While I love practically
all colors, I gravitate to
my favorites and find
new patterns and tex-
tures in those hues. I
group them together
and design possibilities
quickly come to mind.

I collect wrapping supplies all year long, and while none of the items here were purchased together, the blossom pink in the ribbon, paper, and flowers is the common denominator that pulls the look together. Develop your eye by looking for a common thread in the color or motif.

Blue and white looks great every season. **Opposite:** Using Delft blue, I stamped carnations on white freezer paper and tied the package with two widths of ribbon. **This page:** An oversized bow is created with taffeta picot-edged ribbon printed with the recipient's initial and mixed with tulle for a frothy effect.

Opposite: For a late-spring wedding, bridal party gifts were wrapped in blues, celadon, soft greens, and white, reflecting the ferns, blooming flowers, and greenery outside.
This page: Flowers were tucked in at the last minute to be as fresh as possible.

Give your
presents a three-
dimensional look
with a flight
of butterflies
skimming over
a bright yellow
field or a
scattering of
daisies on
cheerful polka-
dot paper.

Katie

Go beyond a simple bow to add dimension to your gifts.
Opposite: Notice how these craft store butterflies unite the ribbon and paper in color and spirit. **This page:** By adding miniature daisies to a polka-dot paper and wrapping the box in tulle, you elevate simple elements into a more exciting whole.

Peonies are so lush and fragrant that they

make any room, table, or gift extraordinary.

Previous pages: Touches of silver balance the feminine pink-and-white palette on a spring table and gift. **This page:** Pick a peony or two to tuck under a ribbon. I grow masses of them in my garden in Connecticut and fill my home with fresh bouquets throughout the season. **Opposite:** While nothing can truly replace the real thing, I was impressed with this silk version that takes the place of a bow.

A gift doesn't have to be a labor of love — but it can look it. **Opposite:** This pretty box took minutes to wrap. Basic white freezer paper is very chic and goes with just about every ribbon or ornamentation. **This page:** A bowl of daffodils heightens the cool, crisp mood of the table.

Inspired by these amazing **blue-and-white eggs from Hungary,** I decorated Easter gifts in **navy-and-white gingham** and added a just-picked blossom.

Happy Birthday
LISA!
May 16, 2005

Be inventive in your
choice of trims.
Opposite: I found this
very inexpensive
mottled paper in New
York City's Chinatown.
The shades are so pure
against moss-green
rickrack and simple
daisies that they
remind me of a perfect
spring morning.
This page: The tag was
printed on the computer
in matching blue ink.

Presents for a
spring wedding.
Opposite: While
these gifts require
some time to make,
they are simple in
terms of technique.
The results of
your efforts will
thrill any bride.
This page: This
beige-and-white
striped gift wrap is
leftover wallpaper
from my office.

Mr. Ed Rollins
requests the pleasure of the company of
Adrian Clear
at dinner to celebrate the birthday of
Carolyne Roehm
Sunday, the sixth of May
at seven o'clock
450 West 31st Street
New York

The lily of the valley is both my birth flower and one of my favorites. **Opposite:** A single stem adorns an invitation to a birthday party. **This page:** This bouquet of faux lily of the valley is a gift within a gift and perfect for May birthdays or a wedding present.

I love the juxtaposition of feminine flowers with tailored stripes and ribbon. **This page:** To put this nosegay with frilly elements might be pretty, but the stripes transform "pretty" into chic. Plus, violets always remind me of the fabulous shopping bags from the old Bonwit Teller store. **Opposite:** Pink and navy is a sophisticated matchup with flowering branches.

Happy Spring
Love Heather

Happy Spring!
May 5, 2005
Love Lily

Classic patterns in pretty hues delight the eye. **This page:** Consider how each of these ribbons would look with striped paper. **Opposite:** A beautiful lilac color and a tiny cluster of lavender flowers soften tailored checks and stripes. The striped paper was made on my computer, which allows me to coordinate the color with any ribbon, flower, or decoration.

I have always believed in the expression, "God is in the details." **Left to right:** The colors of the narrow lavender ribbon and cord match perfectly with the purples and lavenders in the small velvet violets. Gifts can serve as place cards on a spring table. A hand-printed tag tied onto an African violet welcomes guests. Notice how the green ombré ribbon goes with the inexpensive floral paper.

"More than anything I must have flowers

always, always." —*Claude Monet*

Never underestimate the impact of a beautiful gift that shows you've taken the time to create something special.

When I have the time, I like to take the opportunity to wrap gifts in an unusual way. **This page:** Gingham, a favorite fabric of mine, is a perfect material for personalized gifts, especially when made into little pouches and cloth envelopes. **Opposite:** A basket, in any size or shape, is a nice way to present a gift.

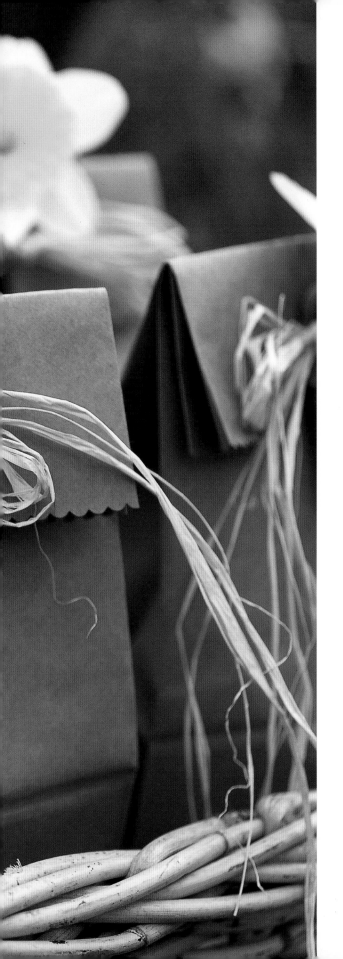

To do something with style and taste does not necessarily require great expense. A simple brown paper bag decorated with raffia and a daffodil is more stylish than the most expensive silk ribbon and gilded paper if they are poorly designed and brashly conceived.

For a spring picnic, both the lunch and the party favors are tucked inside brown paper bags with an assortment of lovely narcissus.

Ah, summer! It's a season of brilliantly colored flowers, sea and sand, entertaining alfresco, and the fun of the Fourth of July. Everything relaxes in the heat of the day. There's a freedom from the constraint and formality of the other seasons that inspires boldness in my gift-wrapping style, allowing me to tuck a sunflower under a striped bow or top a botanical print with a fresh fern. Color and geometry are the predominant themes, contrasting vibrant hues with crisp white in an endless variety of stripes, dots, and checks.

Navy and white is the eternally perfect color combination. In the 1920s, Coco Chanel was inspired by striped mariner's sweaters and made these classic hues the cornerstone of her first collections. It has become our American classic.

This page: This crisp palette pairs well with a flamboyant mix of geometric patterns.
Opposite: I call this look "nautical meets flamenco in a shower of daisies." A daisy is also a geometric design, and these simple flowers act as the punctuation points on a bold package.

THE MARRIAGE
OF
REBECCA AND SAM
AUGUST 13, 1999

ZUCCHINI AND CURRY SOUP
·
POACHED SALMON
WITH A GREEN HERB MAYONNAISE
·
ORZO WITH SUMMER VEGETABLES
·
MESCLUN SALAD WITH FETA
·
WEDDING CAKE

Opposite: For a summer wedding, a bouquet of vibrant fuchsia cosmos, miniature sunflowers, orange marigolds, and blue-violet hydrangea is an explosion of bright color against a gingham tablecloth.
This page: Utilizing some of the same flowers that are in the center-piece, gifts are decorated with small nosegays nestled against striped taffeta ribbon.

For years I have collected blue and white papers and ribbons. Hand-blocked Italian paper works equally well with striped taffeta ribbons, ombré trim, flowers, and raffia.

Summer-sky blue and fluffy-cloud white

work as a perfect backdrop for any color.

This page: Azure is the base color for the "birds of a feather" paper I created on my computer. I dotted the package with fluffy feathers and tied it with a delicate white ribbon that does not overpower the feathers or the script in the quotation.
Opposite: Caribbean blue is one of my favorite summer hues. Hand-printed papers are tied with natural cord and adorned with starfish and seashells to create a sea tableau. The tag was cut from a postcard.

You can never go wrong with red, white, and blue. Betsy Ross knew this when she fashioned the first American flag.

I have a friend who shares the same birthday as our nation. Rather than taking a backseat to this holiday, I say join in and let the Fourth of July be the inspiration for your celebration. Just say the fireworks are intended for you.

Blue and white is a constant theme in all that I design and collect. From creating gardens, interiors, and home collections to collecting porcelain, china, and linens, I never tire of this beautiful combination.

All of the elements of this birthday table are inexpensive but stylish and are unified by the blue and white palette. The mix of carnations, plastic glassware, white plates, and a remnant of striped fabric for the tablecloth create an inviting summer look.

When using gifts to grace the table, don't wrap them all the same way. Select a motif or theme and create variations on that idea. Navy, royal blue, and white are combined with different flowers such as carnations, daisies, and bachelor buttons to distinguish one from another. The variety makes each present special and fun to open.

Flower-bedecked gifts are an essential

part of the table decoration.

Whenever I use brown and white, I think of my late
friend Bill Blass. It was his signature color combination.
This page: Computer-generated checked paper is
tied with grosgrain ribbon and miniature sunflowers.
Opposite: The same paper is combined with a reversible
satin ribbon and a nosegay of brown and white flowers,
creating a graphic medley.

Previous pages: Giant sunflowers and their smaller cousin, the black-eyed Susan, are the perfect blooms for an August birthday celebration. **This page:** Their graphic yellow petals and velvety dark centers look fantastic coupled with bold black-and-white stripes. **Opposite:** The theme is reiterated in the overall decoration down to the details of the invitation and the presents. My friend Sylvia Weinstock made the individual birthday cakes based on my design.

In the language of flowers, the sunflower is an

Please join us
for a Cajun dinner
under the August moon
at Greendune
Saturday, August 4,
2001
8 p.m.

R.S.V.P. Molly 212-753-8012

E. Jewell Jackson McCabe

ideal symbol for my lionhearted Leo friends.

Tropical Fun

This page: Chartreuse works with many colors, but I love it with shocking pink for contrast. Notice how the round shape of the spiky blossom reiterates the dots in the ribbon.

A taste of the tropics is reflected in the sun—

drenched hues of chartreuse and parrot pink.

Opposite: Whenever gifts appear near the table, they become a part of the tablescape and should complement the decorating theme. Tie the wrapping paper, ribbon, or any decorative elements to a color or motif found in the linens, service, or flowers in the centerpiece. **This page:** Hand-blocked Italian paper and an ombré ribbon pick up the verdant hues in the toile table skirt and Venetian glasses.

When the garden is at its peak, there's no better setting for a birthday lunch than among summer's vibrant flowers.

Previous pages: Because of my love of gardening, I collect papers that have a botanical theme. **This page:** When a like-minded friend has a birthday, I acknowledge our mutual interest by incorporating garden elements with my gift.
Opposite: When giving several presents to the same person, I create variations based on a central idea, so each gift has its own identity. The fern and palm papers were purchased, and I combined them with bugs and ferns for more dimension and interest. The olive green paper with the quote was made on my computer.

It's a nice touch to wrap gifts in a manner

that reflects the interests of the recipient.

Food baskets are a nice gift, especially when filled with homemade goodies. **Opposite and above:** Gifts for friends who like to garden are appropriately decorated with faux flowers and ribbons. **Left:** To create distinctive gift containers, I painted a small lunch box and tin pail garden green and trimmed them with checked ribbon and miniature green and brown sunflowers.

I made daisy topiaries that rest in small mossy terra-cotta pots to go with a raffia runner that I bought in France. **Opposite:** Using a second runner, I cut and sewed individual bags to hold party favors for the guests and then tied them with a hemp ribbon and daisies.

Giving your guests a beautifully wrapped party favor that complements the table decoration makes any occasion more festive and helps them feel welcome.

A ticking-stripe paper bag is a great background for blue-and-white striped ribbon and miniature flowers. **Opposite:** I keep an array of colorful shopping bags in different sizes in my wrapping supplies. They are easy to decorate and instantly festive when stuffed with pretty tissue paper and tied with a bow. The birthday greeting was made by printing on acetate and adhering it to the shopping bag.

Autumn is the season of the harvest and the time of year when a stroll down a country lane can inspire countless ideas and projects. I love the change of palette from summer's hot, bright hues to fall's intensely rich tones of red, orange, and brown. Rose hips, bittersweet, bursting chestnuts, autumn leaves, viburnum berries, and acorns are all gifts from nature that provide an endless supply of materials to create beautiful packages for the entire season.

The rich, saturated tones of autumn foliage are at their best when anchored by subtler hues such as burnt umber, moss greens, and earthy browns. **Opposite:** Gather ribbons in varying widths and textures, including stripes and jacquards, in luscious velvet, taffeta, brocade, shimmering satins, and damask.

Halloween was, and still is, one of my favorite holidays, inspiring playful fantasies that allow me to be a kid again.

The changing fall colors in New England always prompt me to invite friends over for an autumn house party. I usually have this weekend event close to Halloween.
This page: Invitations, decorations, and any activities reflect a spooky theme.
Opposite: Spiderwebs cast a spell on a Halloween birthday gift.

Ivy topiaries and garden trellises become the focal points on an elegant autumn table. **Opposite:** An ivy runner and a charming sketch of a Venetian costume are tied onto a gift wrapped in green craft paper. The ivy coordinates with the topiaries decorating the table.

With winter approaching, I find that giving gifts of herbs, ivy topiaries, or a lovely scented plant is a nice way to prolong the summer. Use your imagination so that the presentation is special. Baskets decorated with ribbon, an unusual topiary shape in a clay pot, or a moss bear holding a fragrant jasmine in a silver beaker make these gifts memorable. As you put together your package, take care not to break any of the plant's delicate stems.

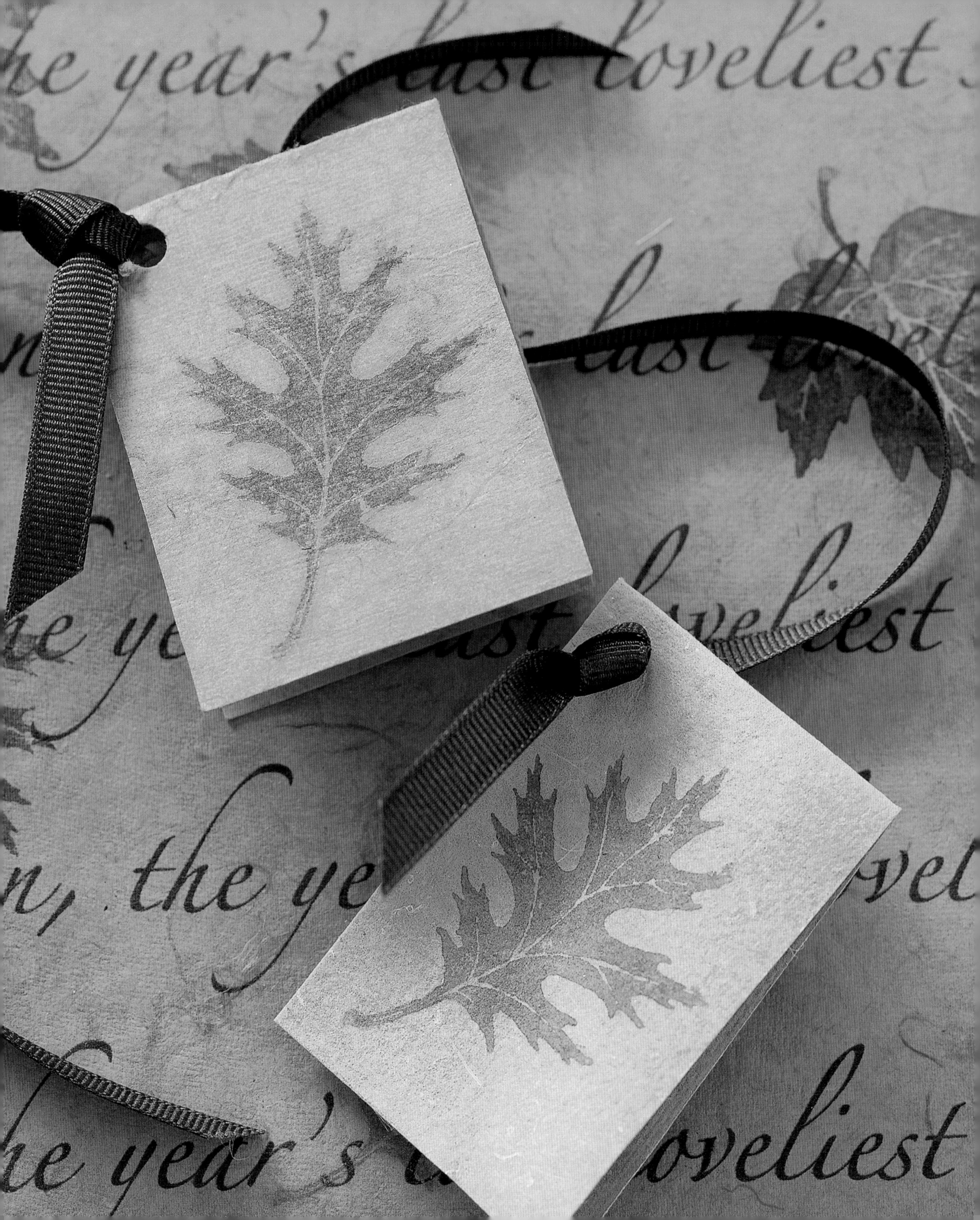
he year's last loveliest
n, the ye
he year's
oveliest

Previous pages: For a last-minute gift for a November celebration, I printed a quote about autumn on handmade papers in warm tones of raw umber, moss green, and burnt sienna.
This page: I over-printed the paper with autumn leaf stamps and tied packages with grosgrain ribbon. Opposite: The same stamps created place cards for the table.

A favorite source of inspiration is the Old Masters. The rich burnt oranges and browns in this postcard of a Bronzino oil are echoed in the bittersweet, oak, and beech leaves atop hand-blocked paper from India. **Opposite:** On the computer, I enlarged a print by Giuseppe Arcimboldo and then pasted it onto russet-colored paper. A drop of sealing wax holds the wax string tied off-center to frame the artwork. A smaller version of the painting serves as the gift card.

Think "outside the box" for beautiful touches. **Opposite:** I tore apart a rather tacky napkin ring that I found in a crafts store, because the glass flowers alone would make a pretty decoration. **This page:** Antique gold spray paint transforms autumn's harvest into elegant extras to put on gifts.

Collecting interesting ribbons is a hobby of mine. **Opposite:** A bouquet of cloth flowers and faux berries plays off a slate blue and natural horsehair ribbon, which picks up the blues in a paper reproduction of an Old Master still life. **This page:** The velvet and taffeta ribbon and a basket of faux rose hips echo the hues in a subtle floral craft paper.

Mixing patterns is a challenge, but done properly, the result is bold and sophisticated. Whenever I give several gifts, I unify a grouping by keeping colors, textures, and patterns in tune with one another. **This page:** To celebrate an impending trip to India, gifts are wrapped in the brilliant colors of that exotic country. **Opposite:** A brocade ribbon from India plays well against a paper with a baroque design.

Bon Voyage
A passage to India
C. R.

Experiment by using different trimmings with the same paper. **This page:** Rich vermilion and scarlet contrast beautifully against brown and white Florentine paper. Brown cotton ribbon and graphic hen feathers make an appropriate gift for a man. **Opposite:** A nosegay of woodcut flowers and striped grosgrain suggest a more feminine style.

A mix of patterns is a way to create

an exciting design that delights the eye.

This imitation shagreen paper is a wonderful replica of that chic material popular in the 1920s art deco period. The embossed velvet ribbon echoes its pebbly texture. **Opposite:** Up close, you can see how the sage leaves, celadon paper, and forest-green ribbon provide a calm palette that contrasts with the rich vermilion flowers.

Carolyn

Creating an interesting gift wrap for a man's present can be a challenge. **This page:** I printed a paper-backed brown tissue with the recipient's initials for a gentlemanly look. Tied with a shiny cord and a bronze ribbon garnished with oak leaves and acorns, a brown-and-gold striped gift fits my definition of masculine. **Opposite:** This package looks appropriate for a man or a woman. Its bottle-green velvet ribbon is embellished with acorns and pinecones sprayed antique gold.

Raffia, straw, hemp, and cord are perfect

Plain or exotic papers get a lift from rustic ties and natural objects. **This page:** An African seedpod found in a dried flower market is the focal point on a leopard-print paper. **Opposite:** Dress up a craft box or plain brown shipping paper with natural packing material, raffia, and a sprinkling of leaves and berries. The gift tag was cut from a manila folder and attached with a narrow hemp cord.

materials for less formal types of gifts.

"Necessity is the mother of invention,"

Home-sewn bags require effort, but the final effect is worth it. **This page:** Two brown-and-white bandannas are stuffed with natural packing material to protect the gift inside. A gingham ribbon and cluster of brown beech leaves ties it up. **Opposite:** A raffia bag is fringed and secured with a bright ribbon and cluster of faux marigolds.

said Plato. No boxes or paper? Bag it!

Winter brings the holidays, which makes it the ultimate season for beautiful gifts. Throughout the year, I collect things to use. As I find a pretty ribbon, a cluster of antique berries, or a vintage Christmas ornament at a flea market, I tuck them away, knowing that when December comes, I'll be prepared. I admit it: I am a gift-wrapping pack rat! Gathering supplies is fun, and it does make this hectic time a bit less frantic. When I open up my cache, I feel like I've given myself a gift of inspiration.

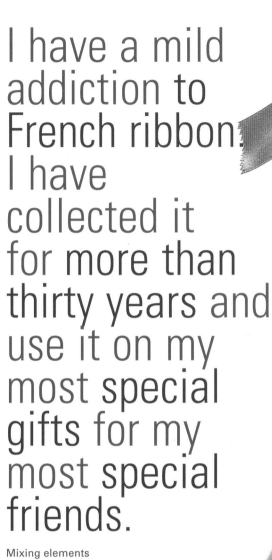

I have a mild addiction to French ribbon. I have collected it for more than thirty years and use it on my most special gifts for my most special friends.

Mixing elements makes a wrapping more interesting. **Opposite:** When I spotted red and green sugar sticks, I thought beyond the tea tray and tied them onto a package for a tea-drinking friend. Note the symmetry of the polka-dot ribbon, the velvet-dotted wire, the balls at the end of the sugar stick, and the round tag with the receiver's initial on it. **This page:** A stack of French ribbons in stripes, plaids, and solid colors.

Taking inspiration from the stately red-and-gold bindings in my library, I decided to decorate both my house and my gifts in a range of those colors.

Burnished gold and a spectrum
of reds from carmine
to vermilion are reminiscent of
Renaissance brocades.

Left to right: I sprayed a variety of leaves, greens, and fruits in different shades of gold and made wreaths, topiaries, and decorations for my gifts with them. Each gift is a variation upon a theme, using red or gold paper and ribbons combined with gilded leaves such as galax, lemon, ivy, and boxwood. I had my monogram made into a stamp to make the gift tags.

A red and gold theme unifies decor and gifts. **Opposite:** The Christmas table holds a vase of red roses and the Rose de Noël. **This page:** Small gifts at each place setting are topped with a rich velvet ribbon, lacquered gold lemon leaves, and a hellebore tucked in at the last minute before guests are seated.

Inspired by the art of the Renaissance,

Gold bags tied with jewel-toned satin and velvet ribbons and golden lemon leaves are adorned with postcards of Old Masters for "his" and "her" gifts.

gifts are wrapped in rich jewel tones.

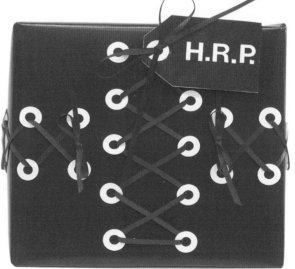

I love mixing stripes of different widths and dimensions—in clothing, in decorative fabrics and wallpapers, in gift wrap, and especially on ribbons, some of which I've had for years. For a red and white Christmas, I used candy-striped paper and ribbons, and then added real candy canes and a fluffy white string for fun. Plain paper, a narrow ribbon, and punch-hole reinforcers create a laced-up package.

Opposite: Collecting red papers, ribbons, tags, art postcards, and decorative items such as fruits, flowers, nuts, pinecones, and stamps will allow you to be inventive. **This page:** At the holidays, a sprig of berries or a tulip-print postcard may not be a traditional adornment, but the lavish red bow supplies the festive note.

I got the idea of using live greens and pinecones on Christmas packages from my Grandma Beaty. I sometimes coat them in artificial snow for a frosty look, spraying the ribbons as well. **Opposite:** A trio of pinecones is a charming detail on a gingham paper stamped with tiny fir trees and finished with a wide contrasting-color ribbon.

Mix up the proportions of your stripes for a striking effect. **Opposite:** Colorful lollipops with their sticks wrapped in matching ribbon are tucked into double bows on a gift. **This page:** Green and red labeling tags carry the first and last initials of the recipient.

Just as in nature, browns and greens are calm and inviting. **This page:** Fir green and rich brown create an elegant backdrop for a cozy fireplace. **Opposite:** The small box on top in Italian marbleized paper is tied with brown satin ribbon and decorated with mixed nuts and greens. The larger box, also wrapped in marbleized paper, holds a taffeta ribbon dressed with preserved oak leaves and pinecones.

Some Christmases, I prefer to use a more natural palette of soft greens and wood tones rather than red and gold.

Soft celadon and moss green papers play off fancy taffeta and satin ribbons and embellishments like seeded eucalyptus, ivy, and faux fruits. **Opposite:** A play of patterns, textures, and a mélange of greens are the elements that make up these elegant, understated gifts.

Mixing similar patterns and tints of a color is a sophisticated approach to gift wrapping. **This page:** Boxes covered in classic Florentine paper are tied in a stack with a muted shade of green satin ribbon, balsam, and miniature pinecones. **Opposite:** When I do not have an appropriate tag or card, I make one out of gift wrap and tie it on with colored string.

My little apartment in Aspen has accents of red
in the decor, so I used red as a prominent color
in my Christmas decorations and on the gifts I
placed around the apartment and under the tree.

Let the decoration of the packages under

the tree reflect the style of your home.

There are times I like to put my presents in gift bags, which are easy to make. **Opposite:** Gingham bows adorn a paper bag bordered with red paper and pinked. A matching tag is stamped with a red reindeer. **This page:** Red gingham is pinked and sewn to form a gift bag stuffed with Christmas tissue and tied with plaid ribbon. The tag is a piece of the tissue backed with white cardboard.

I have always liked the effect of mixing silver and gold. **This page:** To tone down the garish potential of these metallics, I spraypaint natural elements such as leaves, dried flowers, pinecones, and nuts to decorate my gifts. **Opposite:** Mixing different surfaces, elements, and textures in a limited color palette creates a very rich and sophisticated gift.

For a winter birthday celebration, I splurged on exquisite hellebores (or Rose de Noël), a flower dear to my gardener's heart.

Taking my cue from the hellebore's subtle hues, I created bouquets in violets and greens. **This page:** Mixing different greens—moss, chartreuse, celadon, and emerald—makes a more sophisticated arrangement. **Opposite:** Gold paper shimmers under a green satin ribbon and two blossoms.

After the reds and greens of Christmas, I feel the urge to work with a different color palette. **This page:** My first party after the holidays was an ode to blue and white; a miniature orange tree inspired the decoration on the table as well as the gifts. **Opposite:** Citrus hues look sophisticated when paired with dark green paper and ribbon and miniature fruit.

Citrus fruit and tropical
green colors look fresh with
plain white freezer paper.
This page: The tags are made
from botanical postcards.

Icy blue and silver remind me of wintry blue skies as seen through a frosted windowpane.

Tone-on-tone color works when you have a play of textures. **This page:** Mixing ombré ribbon and velvet leaves with silver metallic ribbon and a frosty blue foil paper creates a crystalline wintry look. **Opposite:** Combine different widths of ribbons to tie a generous bow.

Valentine's Day is not just for lovers. It is

Heartfelt gifts.
This page: Pink and red carnations decorate a package for a Valentine's Day celebration.
Opposite: Valentine's Day gifts are placed around vases of pink primulas, ruffled cyclamen, and red azaleas.

also an opportunity to celebrate friendship.

Style is individual, but whatever yours is, tie flowers, decorations, tables, and gifts together to create a look. *That* is real style.

Deep reds and pinks make up the

palette at a Valentine's Day party.

The Valentine's Day boxes I made when I was in the first and second grade inspired this box. **This page:** Construction paper, paper doilies, and crepe paper were the materials of choice. **Opposite:** Cutting bits and pieces of the doily to cover the box and make a gift tag is time-consuming but much like creating a collage.

Children love to unwrap gifts. The excitement they feel as they gaze at what's under the tree or find a birthday present secreted away is enhanced tenfold when gifts are wrapped creatively. One of the joys of childhood, from baby to teenager, is the anticipation of what's inside. As kids tear through the packages on Christmas morning, though, you may ask yourself, "Why bother to make the effort?" But the mysterious allure of receiving a beautiful present meant just for you leaves an impression forever.

Even the smallest amount of effort—using a bright paper or a shiny bow—creates an undeniable effect. Even in their rush to discover the contents of a box, children are not totally oblivious to your efforts. The pains one takes will one day provide a pleasant memory when the gift itself may be long forgotten.

The rustle of tissue paper and gleam of

ribbon heighten the excitement of a present.

This is a direct adaptation of how my grandmother always prepared the cake for my birthday.
Above right: An angel food cake made in a ring pan has a space in the center to hold a small glass filled with spring flowers, in my case usually violets or pansies, as my birthday is in May. **Above left:** Tucked into the ribbon tying the presents would be still more flowers. **Opposite:** For a young friend, I followed my grandmother's tradition but added a moss bear as part of the gift presentation.

As I love West Highland terriers, it was a natural that I would own a Westie stamp, which I used to decorate a plain, pink, glazed paper and to make the gift tag. The white fluffy balls on the wired ribbon remind me of the puppies' coats.

My own love of puppies and pink

inspired this present for a little girl.

Classic men's shirting stripes and tattersal checks make great paper designs for boys.

Above: This cute sailboat trim is perfect for a little boy's gift. I wanted the look of a shirting-stripe fabric, and when I could not find the right width and color, I made it on the computer.
Left: Velum graph paper simulates a tattersal check.
Opposite: A package for the birth of a baby boy was made by using the same computerized stripe and a recycled Easter card that I cut apart and tucked into a blue and gold ribbon.

Stripes are the great equalizer—they look equally appealing when used on gifts for young and old, boys or girls. Their clean, graphic appeal allows you to add on whimsical elements like miniature flowers, gingham ribbon, or multicolor bows.

Modern white daisy stickers, purchased from a craft store, inspire a birthday celebration for a young girl. Instead of place cards, names are computer-printed on acetate, then adhered to the backs of plates and glasses to create gift tags.

I use the daisy motif a lot, as it is such a modern and ageless form and works well with almost any color or design. Using my computer and copying machine, I made the invitation, placemats, and tissue paper napkins and decorated a variety of daisy-inspired presents to make a cohesive theme for a twelve-year-old's party.

It only takes one strong idea or element to spawn an entire theme for a party. **Above left:** Both cloth and paper daisies decorate the table, even topping off the swizzle sticks for the Shirley Temple cosmopolitans. **Above right:** The daisy paper was made by making numerous Xeroxes of the paper daisy sticker. **Opposite and above:** While I Xeroxed the daisy to make paper, tags, placemats, and tissue napkins, if you have a scanner you can create endless designs.

At one point or another, chartreuse and shocking pink seem to be the favorite color combination of about every young girl I know. I still love it! These gifts are all variations upon a theme of geometric shapes on store-bought and computer-generated paper. Mixed with graphic ribbons, sequins, and colored punched-hole reinforcers (close-up, opposite), the overall look is very '60s.

Recycling my paper daisies, I combined them with hot colors in stripes and checks for a young teenage girl who was very much into '60s mod.
Opposite: Avery DayGlo sticker dots change the daisy centers to match the ribbon and give a new look.

Daisies take the place of a bow on

these colorful gifts.

Finding interesting ways to present our gifts is a way to express our creativity, exhibit our thoughts and perceptions about the recipient, and demonstrate our personal style.

A tower of surprises packaged in colorful plastic boxes and filled with shredded cellophane to conceal the gifts will please any teenage girl.
Opposite: Red plastic slicker fabric is sewn into a bag, stuffed with shredded crinkly paper, and tied with satin ribbon. The tag is printed on acetate and backed with the ribbon.

Gingham is a classic pattern (think Raggedy Ann) and used often when designing for little girls. Whether decorated with hand-cut paper dolls (above) or folkloric ribbon and flowers (opposite), it always looks fresh and charming.

I found these Japanese animal plates, cups, chopsticks, and straws in a children's store. The whimsical animal faces in fun colors inspired the wrapping paper and place mats. **Opposite:** Striped ribbon is tied on the gifts, and I color photocopied it to create the stripe on the napkins and tissue paper used inside the boxes.

Even guys like presents more when they

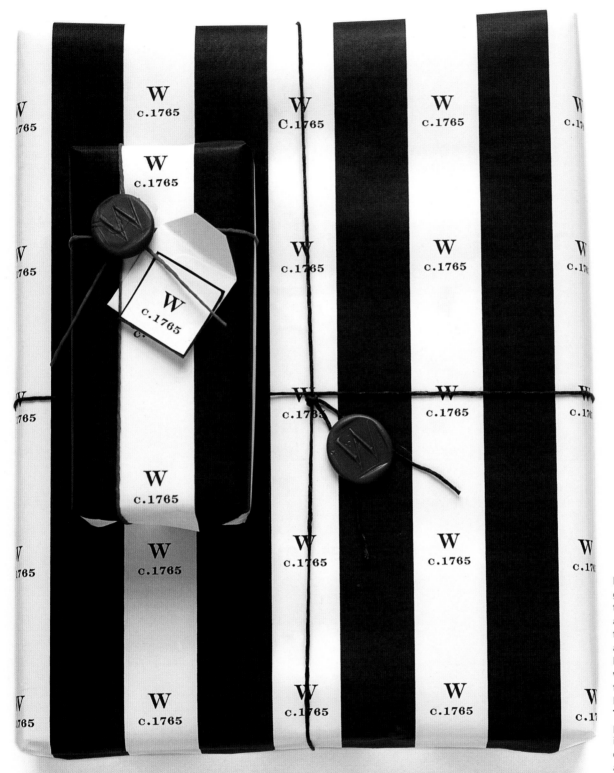

For boys, young guys, and men, I try to make packages that reflect their interests, or an aspect of their lives, such as their work. **Opposite:** For the card player, a lucky hand. **This page:** Stripes, plaids, and checks in masculine colors are always a safe bet.

are personalized and special.

A ribbon printed like a school ruler with a matching tag copied onto acetate makes a great package for any young student.

Black-and-white paper, made on the computer, makes a graphic background to the bright bow. **Opposite:** To make the package more interesting, I photocopied ten inches of the ruler ribbon onto transparent acetate, cut it out, and used it as the gift tag.

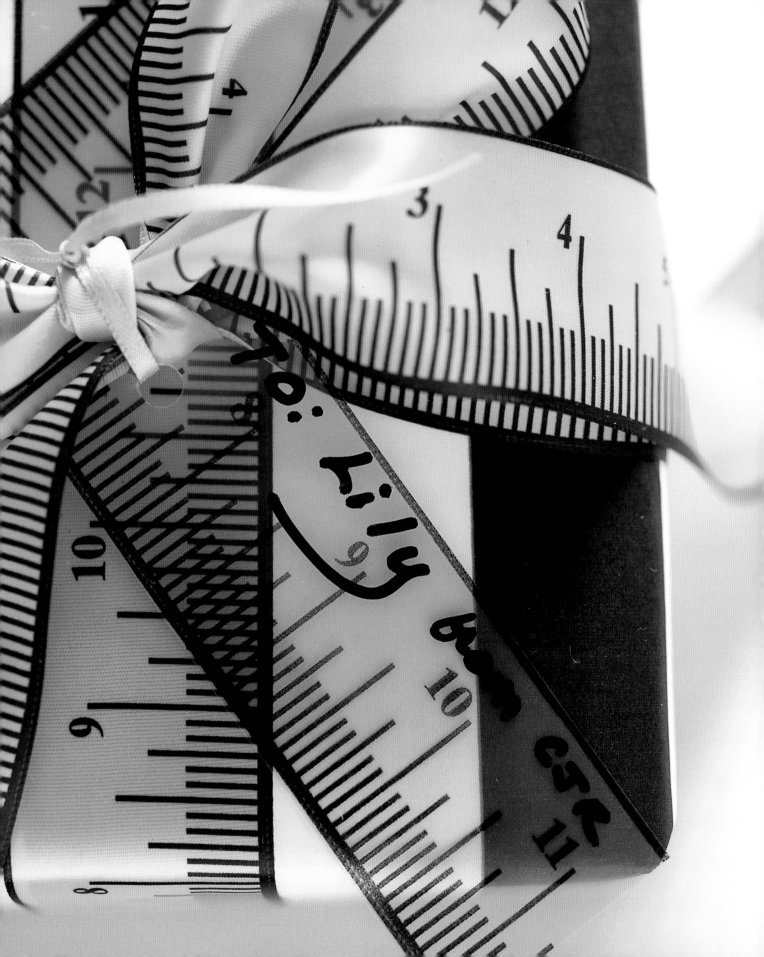

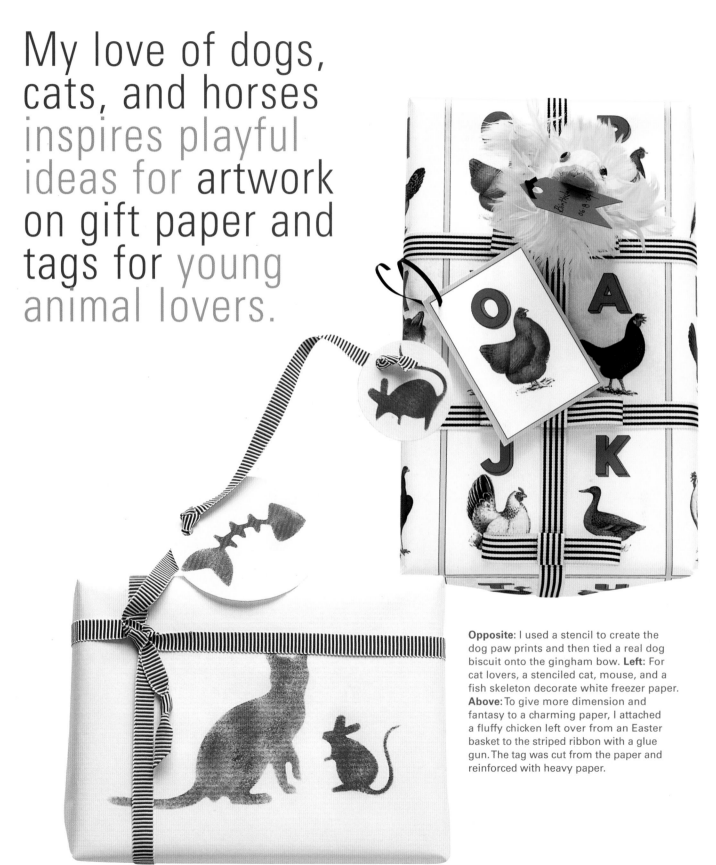

My love of dogs, cats, and horses inspires playful ideas for artwork on gift paper and tags for young animal lovers.

Opposite: I used a stencil to create the dog paw prints and then tied a real dog biscuit onto the gingham bow. **Left:** For cat lovers, a stenciled cat, mouse, and a fish skeleton decorate white freezer paper. **Above:** To give more dimension and fantasy to a charming paper, I attached a fluffy chicken left over from an Easter basket to the striped ribbon with a glue gun. The tag was cut from the paper and reinforced with heavy paper.

A big part of a gift is the care and creativity that go into its presentation. Whether you enjoy gift wrapping or consider it a chore, it will be more enjoyable and infinitely easier if you have the proper tools. I suggest finding a place in your home to store your collection of tools, ribbons, and paper, and having a large surface area to work on nearby to make wrapping easier and faster. At the very least, put together a small box of basic supplies to make the job more efficient and less stressful.

Choosing the right paper, ribbons, and decorations

Papers

Selecting wrapping papers and ribbons is totally subjective. We instinctively choose what we like, but in order to have a small collection of papers that meets your needs, consider these things:

- What are your interests? Are you involved in gardening, sports, traveling, cooking, or reading? Whatever those interests are, look for papers that reflect them.

- What are your favorite colors and color combinations? Have a small assortment of papers (glazed, matte, foil, and tissue paper) in those colors.

- To whom do you repeatedly give gifts? Children, coworkers, family members, women or men friends? Find papers that reflect the gender and age of those people and their relationship to you. Choose paper that reflects a particular interest or hobby of those to whom you send gifts repeatedly.

- On what occasions do you give gifts? Christmas, Hanukkah, birthdays, baby or bridal showers, anniversaries, weddings, Valentine's Day, graduations? Buy papers that relate to the type of giving you do.

- When buying papers for big occasions such as Christmas, try to establish a theme—it will create an impact when you group presents together.

- If you do not feel the need to have themes for gift wrapping, then at least have a few basic colors in good-quality paper, so you are prepared whenever you need to wrap a gift. This saves time (you won't have to rush out to buy paper or ribbon at the last minute) and allows you to be creative.

Paper Basics

- White paper, glazed and matte
- Off-white, ecru, or ivory paper, glazed and matte
- Black glazed paper
- Craft paper
- Gold and/or silver foil
- Your favorite color—in glazed, matte, and/or foil
- Tissue in white and your favorite colors

Ribbon

When buying ribbon, there are several things to consider:

- I suggest that you select your ribbon based on your papers. For instance, I love to garden, so I select a lot of gardening motifs in paper, cards, tags, and decorations. Whenever I see a pretty green ribbon, I will buy it knowing that it will go with one of my garden-related ideas.

- Select ribbons in your favorite color or color combinations.

- I buy all sorts of stripes and dots, as they are patterns I like and ones that I know will mix well with a wide range of other graphics.

- Choose a basic color such as a moss green and then buy it in different materials such as satin, taffeta, velvet, and grosgrain in at least two widths, ranging from 1/8-inch to 3-inch.

- Select either the same color or complementary tones in cords, rattail, raffia, and narrower widths. These are great for attaching tags and cards, and when mixed with wider ribbons help to create texture and a more interesting package.

- If you want to stick with the basics, choose ribbons in your favorite colors, plus a few neutral shades in matte and shiny materials, such as satin and taffeta. With this basic selection, you are prepared for making a beautiful last-minute gift.

Ribbon Basics

- White ribbon in 1/8-inch to 3-inch widths in taffeta, satin, grosgrain, and cotton

- Black ribbon in 1/8-inch to 3-inch widths, in satin, velvet, grosgrain

- Navy blue ribbon in 1/8-inch to 3-inch widths in satin, velvet, grosgrain, taffeta, cotton

- Brown ribbon in 1/8-inch to 3-inch widths in satin, velvet, grosgrain

- A rich red ribbon (a bluish red, not too bright or too orange) in 1/8-inch to 3-inch widths in satin, velvet, grosgrain, taffeta. Red is so basic that it almost works as a neutral.

- Your favorite colors in 1/8-inch to 3-inch widths in satin, velvet, grosgrain, taffeta, organza, cotton, for variety

- Raffia or hemp cord—these are great for more rustic gifts

- Twisted silk or rattail cords in basic and favorite colors

Decoration

My favorite part of gift wrapping is finding interesting and pretty decorative objects to adorn my packages.

As mentioned, my love of flowers and gardens predisposes me to seek out faux flowers made of paper, cotton, velvet, and silk. Fruits, nuts, pinecones, leaves, pods, berries, and some dried flowers are beautiful when incorporated into a gift. I use the term *faux* when describing many man-made items such as silk flowers and branches. This is not an affectation on my part. I simply do not like the terms *fake* or *artificial*. Many of these man-made items are very well done and do not deserve the pejorative connotation that goes along with our English words. The French just sounds a bit nicer!

Other nice elements include miniature Christmas ornaments, shells, miniature toys, candies, art postcards, holiday-oriented objects such as small flags, hearts, Christmas cookies, miniature baskets, charms, and feathers. The list is endless and should include things you like.

In the last few years, an entire industry has cropped up that makes an endless array of miniature objects and stickers with which to decorate cards, scrapbooks, and packages. Most of these are adorable and very well done, but they need to be applied with some creativity in order for them to be effective. If you do not think you are the crafty type or are not interested in making your own decorations, these may be a solution for you.

The Final Word

We all know that wrapping a present prettily is not a necessity. It is merely a small, but thoughtful, gesture that can add to someone's enjoyment of a special occasion. It is a chance to display a bit of our creativity as well. So relax, have some fun, and get pleasure out of your efforts—the nicest gift of all.

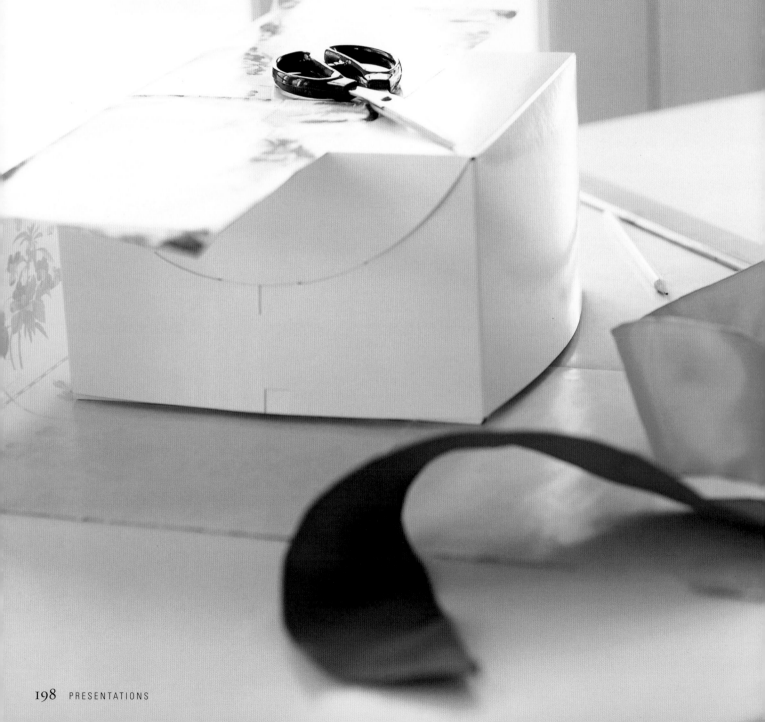

How to wrap the perfect gift

FOLLOW THESE STEPS 1. Pleat two sheets of tissue paper to fit the dimensions of the box you'll be using. Center one tissue north-south, another east-west, and push them down into the box, leaving tissue hanging over the edge on all four sides. Put the gift in the box. Fold the tissue paper edges over the gift. **2.** Measure the wrapping paper against the box (trim the sides of the paper to about three-quarters of the depth of the box) and cut. **3.** Put the top on the box, turn it upside down and place in center of gift wrap. Fold the paper halfway around the box and tape. **4.** Fold under the other raw edge about 1/2 inch. **5.** Affix double-sided tape to the folded edge. **6-7.** Fold the corners as shown and affix with double-sided tape. **8.** Pull paper tight against box to create right angles and a sharp corner. **9.** Repeat the corner folds on the other end of the box.

HOW TO TIE A BOW 1. Wrap the ribbon around the box (as shown). **2.** Tie a knot and cut the ribbon leaving 6-inch tails. **3.** Using two colors of ribbon, form a loop with the ribbon (use half the width of the box to estimate size of loop). **4.** Continue to form loops, pinching in the middle, until four loops are formed on each side (you may have more loops if you are using only one strand of ribbon). **5.** Still holding the pinched center, position the bow on the box knot, and tie the bow onto the package with the ribbon tails. **6.** Gently pull to separate and plump loops. **7.** Trim the ribbon ends on the diagonal. **8.** Punch a hole in the corner of the gift card. **9.** Thread the card onto a ribbon tail.

voilà!

A few basics include scissors, tape, hole punch, stamps, sealing wax, glue, decorative inks, and pens.

What you need

Here is a list of the supplies I keep on hand for wrapping gifts. While you may not want or need everything on this list, the items that are asterisked are necessities. Have these on hand for wrapping gifts at a moment's notice.

GREAT TOOLS TO HAVE
Compass, Paper cutter, Computer,* Printer,* Scanner, Xerox,* Adobe Photoshop, Adobe Illustrator, Embossing tools, Stencils

SCISSORS
Paper scissors,* Ribbon scissors,* Pinking shears, Scallop shears

HOLE PUNCH AND RULERS
Standard size,* Small size,* Assorted styles. An 18" ruler is the most practical.

STAMPS
Assorted designs, Heart, Leaf, Christmas tree, Flowers, Star, Monogram, Letters

INKPADS
White, Gold, Brown, Moss green, Sage green, Bottle green, Sky blue, Navy blue

STICKERS & LABELS
Assorted, Mailing, Avery stickers, Hole reinforcers

TAPE
Double-sided,* Transparent,* Multicolored packing tape,* Black

WRITING TOOLS
Fine point marker,* black & blue,* Red flair,* Gold Marker, broad & fine tip,* Silver marker, broad & fine tip, Fountain pen, Markers, Assorted colors, Colored pencils, Calligraphy pen

SEALS AND WAX
Monogram, Initials, Favorite symbols

SEALING WAX COLORS
Red, Blue, Gold, Green

GLUE
Glue gun, Rubber cement, "Tacky Glue,"* Glue stick,* Pen point glue

TAGS AND CARDS
Plain white tags, Personal cards,* Assorted cards: Christmas, Birthday, Get well, Thank you, Blank, Children, Seasonal tags

Special techniques

Creating your own paper or adding a personalized touch like a flower, card, or creative tag transforms a nice gift into a special one. The following are simple techniques that are fun to do and have memorable results.

Using stamps

Stamps allow you to make decorative papers from plain ones or customize store-bought gift wrap. When stamping a design on paper, follow these steps:

1. Cut paper slightly larger than the gift, allowing yourself a 1- to 2-inch margin.

2. Lightly tape the edges of the paper to a flat surface so the paper does not move when you are stamping it.

3. Plan your design layout and repeat; then, using a ruler and pencil, lightly mark where the center of each motif should be.

4. Apply consistent amounts of ink on the stamp so the impressions look alike.

5. Let the paper dry before wrapping. Note: If stamping on a glazed or foil surface, the drying time is longer than on a matte surface. Make sure all impressions are completely dry before using the paper.

Adding flowers

When I use real flowers on a gift, I tuck them into the box just before I present it—for obvious reasons. Certain flowers such as carnations and chrysanthemums last longer than most flowers. Things to keep in mind:

● Place flowers at the last minute to avoid wilting.

● To keep flowers fresh, you can buy small plastic water picks from a florist supply store, some craft stores, or a florist. Fill the pick with water, place the stem in it, and then cover using the same ribbon as the bow. Start at the top, and wrap ribbon around it in a

barbershop-pole fashion; carefully glue ends in place, then tuck under the bow.

- You can hide the flexible wire stems on faux fruits and flowers a similar way: Twist the stems of the faux flowers or fruit together to form a nosegay. Cover the twisted wires with green floral tape or the same ribbon you are using for the bow, wrapping it around the wires barbershop-pole style. A small dot of glue at each end of the ribbon will secure it.

Making cards & tags

The tag or card you use on a gift can be an important part of the decoration. I save and reuse certain ribbons I like to attach tags I have made to match a paper. While you can find beautiful store-bought tags, it is simple to create your own.

- I often make a tag or card out of the gift paper. I back the paper with cover stock or a heavier weight paper, using spray adhesive, dry mount, or rubber cement to glue them together before cutting to size.

- It's nice to use scalloped-edge scissors or pinking shears for a decorative edge. Make a hole in the corner of the tag using a hole punch so you can string ribbon or cord through it to attach to the gift.

- Postcards make excellent tags. I use a lot of botanical cards and buy art postcards from museum shops.

- Place cards can be used in a pinch as gift tags; mailing tags are also an interesting choice.

- Online clip art is a fun source for creating tags.

- For more modern effects, I like to print tags on acetate rather than paper.

- Novelty items such as plant identification tags, dried or painted leaves, miniature fans, and paper butterflies can make great tags.

- Recycle old greeting cards and Christmas cards by cutting and pasting them to new surfaces.

- Personal photographs make nice cards and tags.

- Of course, stamps make nice tags; you can have your initials cut into a stamp for very little money.

Computer tricks

Making paper on the computer is fun and solves problems when you cannot find a certain color, scale, or pattern that you want.

I love and hate doing this—on the one hand, it is fun, creative, and gives you paper that is yours alone. But it requires a certain level of computer knowledge and skill, of which I have very little, and in order to be really useful, requires a printer that prints, at a minimum, 11- by 17-inch paper. If you are interested in how I made my very simple papers, you can find this information on my website (www.carolyneroehm.com). If you are interested in creating your own patterns, I recommend that you take a few lessons from someone well acquainted with Adobe Illustrator, Photoshop, or Page-Maker and who is very efficient in a word processing program. Believe me, you will have fun and save yourself a lot of frustration.

I have a large-sized printer to make my wrapping paper, but the standard large size paper for most printers is 11- by 17-inches. You can wrap small boxes with that or carefully splice two or more sheets

together to cover a larger box. I do not suggest that you try to do very large boxes this way.

- I like to play on my computer (though this can cause serious bouts of frustration as I am not terribly skillful at it). I have a few fonts that I particularly like to use when making cards, tags, party invitations, and menu and place cards.

- For a more formal look, I use the following: Edwardian Script, Palace Script, ATChevalier, Garamond (several versions), Engravers MT, Didot, and Shelley Allegro Script.

- For less formal ideas, there is Verdana, Zapfino, CarlzMT, Helvetica (several versions), Papyrus, Tahoma, Arial, and Copperplate (several versions).

- You can buy fonts on the Internet or purchase software with fonts from art stores if you wish a larger or more specialized selection.

- I've used Adobe Photoshop or Illustrator to customize the color on the paper to match the color of a bow, set the width of the stripes on a striped paper, and add text that works as a graphic motif as well as a poetic touch on

a gift. The way you put these elements together is by creating layers of images and text. You can design eye-catching type, write a phrase that repeats over the surface of the paper, or create artistic effects such as dry and wet brush strokes, pastel or charcoal drawings. My suggestion to you is to start with a simple technique, like creating stripes using Adobe Photoshop, and experiment from there.

How to create striped paper
Open up the Adobe Photoshop or Illustrator program. Go to the tool bar at the top of your computer to File. Scroll down to New to create a new file for your wrap. A window will drop down to ask you to do the following things: Name your file. Check the size; either by clicking onto a preset Size —I print on 11- by 17-inch paper, but you can also print on 8.5- by 11-inch paper and tape the pages together. The Resolution should be at least 300 pixels/inch. I usually print on white paper.

It's now time to set the background or foreground color. On the right of your screen, you will see a Color menu box. Click on the left box to set the foreground color; the prompt that comes up will allow you to adjust the color to whatever shade you want. Click Okay when the foreground color is correct. You can set the background color in the same way.

Now create your stripes
On the vertical toolbar on the left of your computer screen, you will see a row of boxes. Find the box that is the Rectangular Marquee tool; double-click on that box, draw it to the blank page of your new file, adjust the width of the stripe by starting at the top of the page and drawing the line

down to the bottom. When you click, the color you've chosen for the foreground color should fill the entire stripe with that color.

Repeat the stripe as many times as you want. Print.

How to create paper with a quote
Go through the same steps to create a new file and set foreground and background colors. Go to the vertical toolbar on the left of your computer screen, and scroll down the row of boxes to find the Text tool; double-click on that box, draw it to the blank page of your new file where you want the text to appear, and type your quote, name, or phrase. You can choose the typeface and size of your type by adjusting those settings on the tool bar at the top of your computer.

If you want to repeat the phrase to create an allover effect, you can type the phrase over and over, or create a duplicate layer, which allows you to place the phrase on the page with space between each line. Go to the menu box entitled Layers. Click on the small box of what you've already made and drag it down to the small icon next to Trash, and click on it to create the next layer to work on. Drag the arrow over to where you would like the next word or phrase to be and type it in. Be sure to save your work as you go.

Resources

The following stores are some of my favorite places to find paper, ribbon, and decorative objects for special gifts. Many of these are in New York City, but some have stores across the United States; call or check their websites for other locations.

Ribbon and decorations

B&J Florist Supply
103 West Twenty-eighth Street
New York, NY 10001
212-564-6086

Floral supplies, floral paper, ribbon, spray paints, holiday decorations; tools such as scissors and glue guns; floral wire, vases, decorations such as butterflies, birds, snowflakes, and craft supplies.

Bell-occhio
10 Brady Street
San Francisco, CA 94103
415-864-4048

An extensive selection of exquisite papers, gift wrap boxes (one is shaped like an oyster!), and gorgeous ribbons abound at this Bay Area shop. Stock up on their signature scallop-edged tags and pretty bordered cards.

Black Ink
5 Brattle Street
Cambridge, MA 02138
617-497-1221

101 Charles Street
Boston, MA 02114
617-723-3883

A shop with an eclectic mix of merchandise, plus a wall of wrapping paper, colorful fabric ribbons, and vintage toys to use as gift toppers.

Center of Central Design
145 West Twenty-eighth Street
New York, NY 10001
212-279-5044

Dry and Silk Inc.
123 West Twenty-eighth Street
New York, NY 10001
212-239-3684

Dry Nature Designs, Inc.
129 West Twenty-eighth Street
New York, NY 10001
212-695-8911

Hyman Hendler and Sons
67 West Thirty-eighth Street
New York, NY 10018
212-840-8393
www.hymanhendler.com

High-quality basic, novelty, and vintage ribbon used by the fashion and interior design markets.

M&J Trimming
1008 Sixth Avenue
New York, NY 10018
800-9-MJTRIM or 212-391-9072
www.mjtrim.com

A great resource for ribbon, buttons, trims, feathers, patches and appliqués, tassels, and faux flowers.

Mokuba LLC.
55 West Thirty-ninth Street
New York, NY 10018
212-869-8900
www.jkmribbon.com

High-end ribbons for the fashion and gift markets.

Pany Silk Flowers
146 West Twenty-eighth Street
New York, NY 10001
212-645-9526

Silk Gardens and Trees
113 West Twenty-eighth Street
New York, NY 10001
212-629-0600

So-Good Inc.
28 West Thirty-eighth Street
New York, NY 10018
212-398-0236

Affordable ribbon used by the fashion and interior design markets.

Tinsel Trading Company
47 West Thirty-eighth Street
New York, NY 10018
212-730-1030
www.tinseltrading.com

An excellent source for special ribbon; novelty items such as felt flowers, silk, cotton, velvet flowers and leaves, miniature paper and cloth flowers; plus antique decorative items.

Art, craft, and paper supplies

Container Store
629 Sixth Avenue
New York, NY 10011
212-366-4200
www.containerstore.com

Nationwide chain with paper, ribbon, boxes, containers, and wrapping supplies.

Embrey Papers
11965 San Vincente Boulevard
Los Angeles, CA 90049

This Southern California store known for its elegant stationery also has an incredible selection of gift wrap, including embroidered and handmade papers; grosgrain; doublefaced satin; and hand-dyed silk ribbon from France; plus vintage flowers and letterpress tags.

Kate's Paperie
1282 Third Avenue
New York, NY 10021
212-396-3670
www.katespaperie.com

High-end paper and stationery store, plus craft supplies, ribbon, wrapping paper, cards, tags, and supplies.

Michaels
The Arts and Crafts Store
1-800-MICHAELS or 1-800-642-4235
www.michaels.com

A nationwide chain of craft stores. Check on the website for the location closest to you.

Paper Source
If you're not already familiar with this Chicago-based chain, which has stores in California, Illinois, Massachusetts, Minnesota, Missouri, and Washington, DC, visit the well-stocked website (www.paper-source.com) to find a wide selection of gift papers, from basic to marbled, embossed, and metallic, and Japanese, batik, Indian, and Italian printed wrap. Also available are tags in different shapes and sizes.

Papyrus
1270 Third Avenue
New York, NY 10021
212-717-1060
www.papyrusonline.com

Nationwide chain with beautiful paper, ribbon, and cards.

Pearl Paint
308 Canal Street
New York, NY 10013
212-431-7932
www.pearlpaint.com

Every imaginable art supply you might need, including colored papers, stamps, inks, and paint.

Pearl River Inc.
477 Broadway
New York, NY 10013
212-431-7388
www.pearlriver.com

A store in New York City's Chinatown with decorative papers and exotic add-ons.

Soolip Paperie and Press
8646 Melrose Avenue
Los Angeles, CA 90069
310-360-0545
www.soolip.com

Known as a source for elegant nature-inspired custom wrapping, the store itself is filled with handmade papers (from Japanese Yuzen silkscreen to Parisien Froisse and Cloque); decorative ribbons, twines, pressed natural flowers, sealing wax, and an array of cards.

Talas
20 West Twentieth Street
New York, NY 10011
212-219-0770
www.talasonline.com

A site with decorative papers that include unusual handmade papers; marbleized paper from Spain, France and Italy; reproductions of 1920s designs by the Curwen Press; nineteenth-century floral patterns; and more.

The Store Across the Street
64 West Thirty-eighth Street
New York, NY 10018
212-354-1242

Owned by Tinsel Trading (see above)—more of the same.

Target
www.target.com

This nationwide chain has a nice collection of easily mixed and matched paper products.

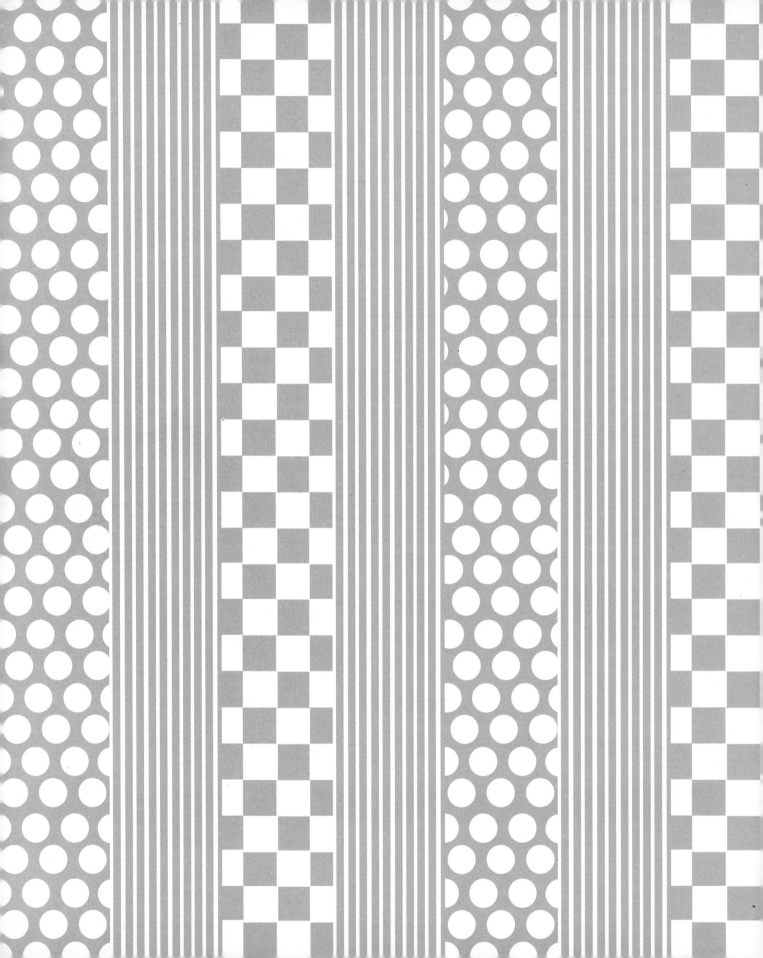